The Drowned World

Gary Owen's first play, *Crazy Gary's Mobile Disco*, was
directed by Vicky Featherstone for Paines Plough and Sgript
Cymru, and toured the UK in spring 2001. His second, *The
Shadow of a Boy*, was produced by the National Theatre in
June 2002 and was joint winner of the George Devine
Award. *The Drowned World* opened in August 2002 at the
Traverse Theatre (Paines Plough). His first Welsh play,
Amser Canser, will be produced by the Welsh College of
Music and Drama early in 2003. Gary's first radio play,
The Island of the Blessed, was broadcast in July 2002 as part
of *The Wire* on BBC Radio 3.

by the same author

Crazy Gary's Mobile Disco
The Shadow of a Boy

The Drowned World

Gary Owen

Methuen Drama

Published by Methuen 2002

Methuen Publishing Ltd
215 Vauxhall Bridge Road
London SW1V 1EJ

www.methuen.co.uk

Copyright © 2002 by Gary Owen
The author has asserted his moral rights.

Methuen Publishing Ltd reg. number 3543167

ISBN 0 413 77282 9

A CIP catalogue record for this book is available at the British Library

Typeset by SX Composing DTP, Rayleigh, Essex
Transferred to digital printing 2004

Caution

painesPLOUGH in association with Graeae present

THE DROWNED WORLD

by Gary Owen

First performed at the Traverse
Theatre 1 August 2002

Note: The playscript that follows was correct
at time of going to press, but may have
changed during rehearsal.

THE DROWNED WORLD
by Gary Owen

Cast *(in order of appearance)*

Darren	Neil McKinven
Tara	Josephine Butler
Kelly	Eileen Walsh
Julian	Theo Fraser Steele

Director	Vicky Featherstone
Designer	Neil Warmington
Lighting Designer	Natasha Chivers
Composer and Sound Designer	Nick Powell
Assistant Director	Jamie Beddard
Production Manager	Simon Sturgess

Company Stage Manager	Dawn Rawcliffe
Technical Stage Manager	Gary Morgan
Sign Language Interpreter	Jeni Draper
Audio Describer	William Elliott
Press Representative	Emma Schad
Graphic Designers	Eureka! Design Consultants Limited
Cover Photography	Sheila Burnett

With thanks to:
Jenny Sealey, Roger Nelson, Claire Saddleton, Michael Fraser, Zoe Squire, Ben Jeffries and Miuccia Prada.

GRAEAE AND THE DROWNED WORLD

Following on from the recent success of *Wild Lunch VI* – a new writing project with both disabled and non-disabled writers, actors and directors that was Paines Plough and Graeae's first collaboration – The Drowned World seemed the natural next step as the two companies continue to share expertise.

Jamie Beddard was awarded an Arts Council of England bursary in 2001 to train with Graeae as a director. Having worked on Wild Lunch as both writer and project co-ordinator, Graeae is delighted that Jamie has been invited back to Paines Plough as Assistant Director for The Drowned World.

This production also includes a week of performances accessible to sensory impaired theatregoers, through sign language interpretation and audio description, backed up by supporting information in accessible formats: large print/Braille programmes, synopses, taped notes and introductions, etc.

This is a toe in the water, but an important part of an on-going collaborative investment between Graeae & Paines Plough, which aims to result in a full-blown co-production involving disabled performers and members of the creative team, and, for people with physical and sensory impairments, full access at all performances.

THE COMPANY

Gary Owen
Writer

The Drowned World is Gary's third stage play. His first, Crazy Gary's Mobile Disco, was produced by Paines Plough and Sgript Cymru, and toured Great Britain in spring 2001. His second, The Shadow of a Boy, was directed by Erica Whyman as part of the National Theatre's Transformation season in June 2002. Gary's first full length radio play, The Island of the Blessed, went out in July 2002 as part of The Wire on Radio 3. In 2001, Gary was Paines Plough's Writer-in-Residence, a post supported by the Pearson Playwrights' Scheme and the Peggy Ramsay Foundation. In 2002, he was joint winner of the George Devine Award for Most Promising Playwright. Gary's fourth stage play - and his first in Welsh - will be produced by Sgript Cymru and the Welsh College of Music and Drama early in 2003.

Jamie Beddard
Assistant Director

Jamie Beddard has worked as an assistant director on Peeling (Graeae) and co-director on The Devil of Great Titchfield Street (as part of Paines Plough/Graeae's Wild Lunch VI season).

As a writer Jamie has produced: Walking Among Sleepers (Jo Rawlinson & Caroline Parker); A Fading Light (Paines Plough/Graeae) and Life Support (Soho Theatre/Writernet).

Josephine Butler
Tara

Josephine trained at the Webber Douglas Academy of Dramatic Art. Theatre work includes: Hock and Soda Water (Chichester); The Blue Room and Watching the Sand from the Sea (Derby Playhouse); Ghost Sonata and Storm (Gate).

Television work includes: Fifteen Storeys High; Second Sight; Dalziel and Pascoe (BBC TV). The Raven (Gaumont TV); Blonde Bombshell (LWT); Mr White Goes to Westminster (Hat Trick); The Vanishing Man (ABTV); Going Wrong (Meridian), Wycliffe (HTV) and Bliss (Carlton UK).

Film work: Lawless Heart (Mp Productions). Shiner (Wise Croft Film); Sleep (Airship Films); Charity (Portobello Films); Out of Depth (Steon Films) and Up Stood the Ape (Dum Dum Films).

Natasha Chivers
Lighting Designer

For Paines Plough: Helmet (also Traverse Theatre); Tiny Dynamite (also Frantic Assembly, Contact); Crazy Gary's Mobile Disco (also Sgript Cymru). Other work includes: Among Unbroken Hearts (Traverse Theatre/ Bush Theatre); A Chaste Maid In Cheapside (Almeida); 1001 Nights and The Firebird (Unicorn Theatre); Life with An Idiot (The Gate Theatre); A Listening Heaven (Royal Lyceum Theatre, Edinburgh); Eliza's House (Royal Exchange Theatre Manchester); Notre Dame De Paris (Strathcona Theatre Co

- tour/Lyric, Hammersmith); Hammerklavier (Theatre de Nesle, Paris) and Sweet Phoebe (Sydney Festival 2002); Sell Out and Hymns (Frantic Assembly); Buried Alive and Demons and Dybbuks (Young Vic for Method and Madness).

Site specific theatre, recent work includes; Caledonian Road (Almeida); Mapping the Edge (in sites across Sheffield –WilsonWilson Company/Sheffield Crucible);Ghost Ward and Into Our Dreams (Almeida Site Specific Projects), Mincemeat at The Old Hartley's Jam Factory (Cardboard Citizens); The Salt Garden (Strathcona at the National Maritime Museum; Greenwich) Waving (Oily Cart in Hydro-therapy pools/tour).

Future work includes: Peepshow, a new musical for Frantic Assembly.

Jeni Draper
Sign Language Interpreter

This is Jeni's first show with Paines Plough although she was one of the interpreters on Wild Lunch VI a joint Paines Plough/Graeae series of play readings at the Young Vic in May 2002.

As an actress, she has worked extensively in theatre, TV and film.

Work includes: The Changeling (Graeae); Into the Mystic (Graeae); Mountain Language (In Tandem); Message in a Bottle (Graeae); Squeelin like a Pig (Oxford Touring Theatre Co); Jane Eyre (Channel Theatre Co); Don Quixote de la Mancha (Show of Hands); Up n Under (Trinity Theatre); All's Well That Ends Well (Theatre Set up); As You like it (Chelsea Centre/Garrick); The Bill (Carlton);

Eastenders; Dear Dilemma; Murder Without Motive (BBC;) Symbiosis (RCA) and A Short Trip (Gangster Productions).

Vicky Featherstone
Director

Vicky Featherstone is Artistic Director of Paines Plough. For Paines Plough: Tiny Dynamite by Abi Morgan (co-directed by Scott Graham and Steven Hoggett; Crazy Gary's Mobile Disco by Gary Owen, Splendour by Abi Morgan (TMA/Barclays Theatre Award for Best Director), Riddance by Linda McLean, The Cosmonaut's Last Message To The Woman He Once Loved In The Former Soviet Union by David Greig, Crave by Sarah Kane, Sleeping Around by Stephen Greenhorn, Hilary Fannin, Abi Morgan and Mark Ravenhill, and Crazyhorse by Parv Bancil.

William Elliott
Audio Describer

William began his foray into audio description last year when he toured with Graeae Theatre Company, describing their production of The Changeling. He has also described at the Palace Theatre Watford in The Deep Blue Sea and Take Me Out at the Donmar Warehouse. In December of this year he will be at the Palace Theatre in the West End, describing a performance of Les Miserables.

Theo Fraser Steele
Julian

Theatre Work includes: Importance of Being Ernest (Savoy/International Tour); Skylight (Vaudeville/National Tour); The Shallow End (Royal Court/Duke of York's); A Week with Tony (Finborough); Amphitryon (Gate); Tamburlaine the Great (RSC/Barbican).

Television includes: Keen Eddie (Paramount); Close and Innocent (United Broadcasting and Entertainment); A Christmas Carol (Hallmark); The Prince of Hearts (BBC Screen One); The Visitor (Tiger Aspect).

Radio Includes: Skylight; The Green Gage Summer and Antoine et Dougie (BBC Radio 4).

Film Includes: Before You Go (Pacifus/Big Fish); Mad About Mambo (Polygram); Mrs Brown (Ecosse Films); When in London (Mad Hatter Prods); Waterland (Palace Pictures).

Neil McKinven
Darren

Theatre includes: For Paines Plough: Riddance; The Cosmonaut's Last Message to the Woman He Once Loved in the Former Soviet Union. A Midsummer Nights Dream (Brunton); Glen Gary Glen Ross; Woyzeck; Dead Funny (Lyceum, Edinburgh); Wiping My Mothers Arse; Abandonment; Fire in the Basement; Widows (Traverse Theatre); Macbeth (Aberdeen);Oedipus (Theatre Babel); A Family Affair (Number One Tour); Dissent, Caledonia Dreaming and Road (7:84); Afters (Gilded Balloon, Edinburgh); The Mark (Cockpit); The Ship (Glasgow Docks); Underwater Swimming (New End); When I Was a Girl I Used to Scream and Shout (Commercial Tour).

TV includes: A is for Acid (Granada); Taggart (STV); Glasgow Kiss; Rab C Nesbitt; The Vet; Degrees of Error ; Takin' Over The Asylum; Straithblair and The Ship (BBC).

Film; Lost and Commission (Academy Films).

Nick Powell
Composer and Sound Designer

Nick has been working as a musician since 1990. For Paines Plough; Tiny Dynamite, Splendour, Riddance, The Cosmonaut's Last Message.., He has toured and recorded with various bands including Strangelove (EMI Records), Astrid (Nude Records), Witness (Island Records) and Speeka (Ultimate Dilemma). His screen work includes several short films as well as soundtracks for Channel Four (including BAFTA award winner 'Beneath The Veil': Best Current Affairs program 2002), ITV, BBC World Service, Sky One and CBS in the US. As Musical Director of Suspect Culture - a theatre company formed in collaboration with Graham Eatough and David Greig - he has scored and been part of the development of eight shows including Airport, Timeless, Mainstream, Candide 2000, Casanova and this year's Lament, as well as numerous workshops and performances in Britain, throughout Europe and, recently, in Sao Paulo, Brazil. Through the British Council, he has worked with Teatro De La Jacara in Madrid, Bouge-de-la and The Max Factory and will be touring later this year with Improbable Theatre. He is one half of the duo OSKAR who worked with Vicky Featherstone on three shows for PRADA in Milan, and have several CD releases in progress.

Simon Sturgess
Production Manager

Simon has worked as a Stage and Production Manager with many Theatre Companies including The Gogmagogs, Cheek by Jowl, Nigel Charnock + Company, Frantic Assembly, Lyric Hammersmith, LIFT, Dukes Theatre Lancaster, Greenwich Theatre, Music Theatre London, Theatre Royal Stratford East, Die Kammerspiele (Hamburg) and Not the National Theatre.

This year he has been Production Manager of a variety of events and conferences as well as Actors' Touring Company's Arabian Night and Graeae's Peeling, both of which had runs at the Soho theatre following national tours.

This is the first time Simon has worked with Paines Plough.

Eileen Walsh
Kelly

Theatre Work includes: For Paines Plough; Crave by Sarah Kane and Splendour by Abi Morgan. Troilus and Cressida (Oxford Stage Company); Boomtown (Rough Magic/Dublin Theatre Festival); Disco Pigs (The Bush/Arts Theatre); Phaedra's Love (Corcadorca); Danti Dan (Rough Magic/Hampstead Theatre).

Film work includes:Nicholas Nickleby (Douglas McGrath); Getalife.com (Enzo Cilenti); Magdelane (Peter Mullen); Miss Julie (Mike Figgis); Janice Beard 45 WPM (Claire Kilner); The Last Bus Home (Jonny Gogan); Spaghetti Slow (Valerio Jalongo) and The Van (Stephen Frears).

Neil Warmington
Designer

For Paines Plough: Helmet (also Traverse Theatre); Splendour; Riddance; Crazyhorse. For Traverse Theatre: Gagarin Way; Wiping My Mothers Arse; Family; Passing Places; King of the Fields ; Full Moon for a Solemn Mass (also Barbican Pit). Other work includes: Marriage of Figaro (Garsington Opera); Desire Under the Elms; Jane Eyre (Shared Experience); Don Juan; Love's Labours Lost; Ghosts; King Lear; Taming of the Shrew (English Touring Theatre); Dissent; Angels in America (7:84); Woyzeck; The Glass Menagerie; Comedians (Royal Lyceum, Edinburgh); Life is a Dream; Fiddler on the Roof (West Yorkshire Playhouse); The Duchess of Malfi (Bath Theatre Royal); Henry V (Royal Shakespeare Company); Much Ado About Nothing (Queen's, London); The Life of Stuff (Donmar Warehouse); Much Ado about Nothing; Waiting For Godot (Liverpool Everyman); The Tempest (Contact, Manchester); Women Laughing (Watford); Troilus & Cressida (Opera North); Oedipus Rex (Connecticut State Opera). His awards include: 3 TMA Awards for best design (Life is a Dream; Passing Places; Jane Eyre); The Linbury Prize for Stage Design,The Noel Machin memorial painting prize and The Sir Alfred Munnings Florence Prize for painting.

PAINES PLOUGH

"this is surely the bright new future of theatre" Independent

The driving force behind Paines Plough is the vision of the playwright and the company has been discovering outstanding new voices in British theatre since 1974. Funded by the Arts Council of England we seek, encourage, develop, support and produce writers nation-wide, touring a minimum of two new plays a year throughout the UK and presenting regular rehearsed readings by writers with varying levels of experience.

In 1997, Paines Plough appointed its sixth Artistic Director - Vicky Featherstone. Since Vicky's appointment, Paines Plough has gone from strength to strength making it one of the most respected theatre companies in Britain today.

At every level, writers are encouraged to be courageous in their work, to challenge our notions of theatre and the society we live in.

Since 1997 Paines Plough has produced: TINY DYNAMITE by Abi Morgan (MEN Best Fringe Production), CRAZY GARY'S MOBILE DISCO by Gary Owen, SPLENDOUR by Abi Morgan (TMA Barclays Theatre Award Best Play and Best Director, Fringe First and a Herald Angel 2000), RIDDANCE by Linda McLean, (Fringe First and a Herald Angel 1999), THE COSMONAUT'S LAST MESSAGE TO THE WOMAN HE ONCE LOVED IN THE FORMER SOVIET UNION by David Greig, CRAVE by Sarah Kane, SLEEPING AROUND by Hilary Fannin, Stephen Greenhorn, Abi Morgan and Mark Ravenhill, CRAZYHORSE by Parv Bancil and THE WOLVES by Michael Punter.

Wild Lunch
Wild Lunch is a regular Paines Plough festival of script-in-hand performances, born out of a selected writers group, the latest, Wild Lunch VI was a co-production with Graeae Theatre Company and culminated in a festival in May 2002 at the Young Vic.

This Other England
Paines Plough was awarded Peggy Ramsay Theatre Company of the Year 2001 for THIS OTHER ENGLAND, a three year project of full length plays by some of the country's most prominent and innovative playwrights. The writers are Simon Armitage, Biyi Bandele, David Greig, Linda McLean, Abi Morgan, Philip Ridley, Peter Straughan, Naomi Wallace and Enda Walsh.

The plays written for THIS OTHER ENGLAND will share the theme of the development of the English language over the last thousand years. Our ambition is for the nine plays to create an alternative census of Britain at the beginning of the 21st century.

PAINES PLOUGH - COMPANY

Artistic Director	Vicky Featherstone
Associate Director	John Tiffany
General Manager	Caroline Newall
Literary Associate	Lucy Morrison
Adminstrator	Susannah Matthews
Writer In Residence	Ursula Rani Sarma

PAINES PLOUGH BOARD OF DIRECTORS

Roanna Benn; Tamara Cizeika; Ian Codrington (Company Secretary); Giles Croft; David Edwards (Chair); Chris Elwell (Vice Chair); Jenny Sealey

Education. Paines Plough offers a variety of workshops and teaching materials. If you would like more information about our education work please contact Susannah at Paines Plough or look on our website.

Mailing List. If you would like to be on Paines Plough's free mailing list please send your details to:

Susannah Matthews
Paines Plough
4th Floor
43 Aldwych
LONDON WC2B 4DN

T + 44 (0) 20 7240 4533
F + 44 (0 20 7240 4534
office@painesplough.com
www.painesplough.com

The Drowned World is supported by Graeae, Madeline Barnes, Carl Dowling, The Wild Family and The Barnes Family.

 are supported by:

My thanks to all at Paines Plough, to the Pearson Playwrights' Scheme for giving me the time to think my way into this one and to Michael McCoy.
Diolch o galon i ti, Catrin.

for Vicky Featherstone

Julian *and* **Tara** *carry themselves as if they are radiantly beautiful.*
Darren *and* **Kelly** *do not.*

Darren   I get to the station with still some hope left.
I climb to the platform, and I have still some hope left: hope
for a moment of lightheadedness, a surface slippery and wet,
A loss of balance, an unexpected meeting of mind and
escalator.
No such luck.
I make it to the train intact.
I find a seat. I sit down.
The faces around me stretch and settle into a protective
blankness and –
Ahead of me, a foot stretches out.
It stretches from the toe, lifting off the ground into the air,
pointing, pulling the rest of the leg into line behind it. The
skirt draped around the leg falls away, it falls away along the
line of a split that goes right up to the thigh, and I see toe
and foot and calf and thigh stretched out, and even though I
can't see her face, from watching the muscle define itself in
the underside of her calf it's as if I'm looking into her eyes,
drinking in her lazy, luxuriant pleasure in the sensation of
the tendons tightening all along her leg.
Her hand reaches down, and pulls the skirt back over the
thigh as the leg relaxes and lowers itself back to the floor.
At the next stop I stand, turn away from her, walk through
the carriage and get off the train at the far end. I walk along
the platform to the doors just in front of her, and hop back
on.
I sit down opposite her. I don't meet her eyes as I sit.
I can't.
I don't need to.
I watch her reflection reading a paperback as the train
flashes past towns and villages and the people and the lives,
the worlds within them –
– all these worlds glide under the surface of her skin, she
contains whole worlds within her.
Whole worlds I could escape into.
I watch her reflection in the window and I know –

– she is the angel sent to save me.

The train draws into the East Central Station and I don't move.

I don't join the crowds of suits and students bustling to get off. I sit there and so does she. I wait for her to lean over and gently touch me on the arm and say something simple and beautiful, maybe just say hello and suggest we go for a coffee or a drink at some café I've never noticed before, tucked in one of these arcades I always hurry through.

We'll sit down. She'll have a mineral water and smile indulgently as I order a crisp German beer. I'll explain that in her absence it has become my habit to take a reviving draught of lager at around ten each morning. She'll let me get away with it but her smile will be saying – six months and I promise, you won't be needing that rubbish in your system . . .

I sit and wait for her to make her move and she puts away her book and looks up and I look up and finally our eyes meet and she –

– this angel smiles at me –

– and she stands and goes to the door and gets off the train. She walks along the platform, down the stairs and away into the crowd.

Beat.

I see her again as I'm walking to work, of course.

I see her in a blonde waving high denomination notes at a cabman outside the station.

I see her in a brunette sat on a number 18 bus pulling into Wood Street.

I see her in this thin, elf-faced girl sitting drinking coffee at the Hayes Island Refreshment Bar who looks for all the world like a perfectly lit kinograph star –

I see her again and again and each time as I pass I focus my mind and send a telepathic burst saying – here I am, here I am, I'm the one you've been sent to save so now *turn around* –

– and say hello or touch my arm or smile and we can just take it from there, please. Please.

Just one moment of warmth, please. Just one graspable moment. One instant of care I can refer back to in times of unease or discomfort. Something to be an anchor. To keep me from drifting off. To keep me from sliding under. To – Obviously I'm not saying I'm anything special – I'm of course entirely ordinary but ordinary people don't have to struggle on month after month after month without a kiss or a cuddle or a smile smiled for them and them only –

Beat.

– I'm being brushed past, I'm receiving glancing blows –
– to my elbows and my back –
– and I can't bear even the least impression of these people –

Beat.

I realise my mistake.
The angel is coming *for me*.
I don't have to go looking for her.
She's going to come for me.

Beat.

That was the last time I set foot outside.

Tara   I tread water, just below the surface of sleep.
I float there for as long as I can.
I'm like a body trapped in the ribs of a shipwreck.
When I wake the seabed shifts, the body is set free and the gases of decay send it shooting through the surface.

Kelly   I'm up today hours before I need to be.
I doze off easily enough, but sleep can't keep a hold on me.
At dawn I give up.
I go down to the harbour. I sit on the quay and watch the grey waves, rolling off the horizon, battering themselves against the sea walls.

Tara   When I wake, when I fall up through the surface of sleep, his arms are there to catch me.
His arms mark out the limits of the world: the world's breath warms the back of my neck; its fingers gently stroke

my hair; the world loves me.

These are the moments I will try to remember when I find myself . . . polishing a window or pruning a rose bush in the garden and without warning I appreciate the sheer ridiculousness of carrying on. When it strikes me that I could be preparing to slip away under the cover of the night, I could be obtaining false papers, – and instead, I'm washing clothes. Polishing windows. Pruning rose bushes.

When the sheer ridiculousness of it all overwhelms me, I'll be tempted to take the shears, and hack into the plant, to hack it ragged, to sink the shears in and watch its sap ooze out, watch its heartwood dry out and die in the sun.

I'll resist that temptation. I'll remember those first few moments of the day, when the world loved me. And I'll prune the rose bush. I'll pick moss out of the lawn. I'll weed the herb garden, and breathe in the mint and the rosemary. I'll do these things aware that tomorrow the whole place might be doused in petrol.

Because they would.

They will.

They'll burn the garden. They'll see we care about it and so they'll burn it.

Once they've finished with the house.

Before they start on us.

Kelly   Walking back into the heart of the city, I see a kid. Eight, nine years old, on this ragged old horse, riding bareback, clinging onto its mane.

There's a smile in his eyes.

A shout of pleasure forming in his mouth.

No citizen would dare be out of doors, breaking curfew.

No citizen would ride like he owns the street. Like the city is his.

Beat.

I reach inside my jacket. I click open my holster.

Tara   I couldn't wake alone.

I couldn't do for him what he does for me.

I can't imagine how anyone could.

What must be in his heart, that he can take all this and still have strength left to comfort me.

Kelly   The leather of the holster gives the slightest creak, surely too soft a sound to carry – but as my hand curls around the grip of my pistol, he becomes aware of me.
He becomes aware he's being looked at.
The smile dies on his face. And his eyes are sunken, his mouth twisted and sulky, muscles under his cheeks withered. My gaze slides off him.
He's one of us. He's a citizen.
I wave, so he'll see my hand is empty, and understand he's in no danger.
I wave, but I can't bear to look at . . . that mouth, those eyes.
The pony's hooves crack on the cobblestones as the boy gallops away.

Tara   We lie in bed, holding each other, and Julian tells me stories about what we're going to do with the day.
We'll get up, wash, get dressed; we'll make breakfast and then do the breakfast dishes, and so on and so forth; we talk the day out, we talk through every detail so we can see it stretching ahead of us.
You see, he tells me, they can't come today. Because –
There are so many things that need doing today – we simply haven't got *time* for them to come.
And so we get up: like citizens.
We get on with the day, like citizens.

Kelly   I pick up my squad from the barracks. One with oozing skin, one with ruined teeth.
I lead them through the city. They're excited: chattering like schoolchildren behind my back.
They've never carried out a quarantine order before.

Tara   They won't come for us today, like they didn't come for us yesterday.

Kelly   We stand for a moment outside the house.
It seems deserted.
But perhaps they're just asleep.

I wonder if they do sleep.
Or if they just go to bed, and lie there, waiting.

Tara   Except.
I've taken the loaf from the bread bin. I've put it down on the table. I've gone to the drawer and I'm pulling the bread knife from the drawer and –

Kelly   Knock knock.

Tara (*to* **Julian**)   Who's that?

Beat.

Julian   When the world started to end
I have to admit,
I was glad.
It was a relief.
I felt at home, at last.
It wasn't that I had found my place
It was that when the world cracked
A place for me was created in it
A purpose. A role.

Kelly   Knock knock.

Tara *looks at* **Kelly**.

Julian   Don't worry: I promise you.
It's not them.
They haven't come for us.
It's just –

Kelly   Just kids.

Julian   It'll just be kids. Trying to panic us.
So don't give in to them.
Don't give them what they want.

Kelly   They're just kids.

Beat.

Neither of them a day over eighteen.
Ruined teeth and oozing skin.

Waiting for me to give the order.

Julian (*beat*)   The idea was to go with some dignity.
To keep some dignity about us, for as long as that was
possible.
When they came we would just –
– we wouldn't resist.
We wouldn't make a fuss or try to escape.
We wouldn't offer them any kind of distraction.
We would let them focus on what they had come to do.
And we hoped /
/ I hoped, if they saw clearly what they were doing –

Kelly   Oozing skin and ruined teeth, they can't wait to get
down to business.

Julian   What I did wrong was –
I went to the window.
Just in case. Just to check.

Beat.

It wasn't seeing the soldiers tht made me doubt.
It wasn't the hooks, or the gloves, or the rope. It wasn't the
little tub of paraffin or the tindersticks, for setting light to
our bodies afterwards.
It was the officer. It was the sheet of paper in her hand. The
quarantine order.
No matter how little noise we made. No matter how much
time and space we gave them to think, there would be the
quarantine order telling them: ignore any queasiness or
shortness of breath. These reactions can be distressing, but
are entirely normal. Carry on with your duty, and these
physical pangs will soon correct themselves.

Beat.

They're not a confident people.
I hoped they might have been persuaded.
On an individual level.
I was sure they could be.
But they came with a piece of paper. An order. Giving clear

instructions on how to deal with the bodies.
I hadn't thought of that.

Tara   I remember the moment.
He went to the window, pulled back the drape and
He didn't move, he didn't jump
But he seemed to flicker.
He seemed to not quite be there.

Kelly   Later, the inquisitor asked me about the initial
moment of exposure.
I told him: the house was dark, the curtains drawn. I
remember looking at my reflection in the window, and the
curtains parted, and there was a man's face on the other
side of the glass.
The inquisitor asked, what physical sensations were
experienced at this time? I said: I felt sick. I felt like the
insides of my stomach had gone missing.
The inquisitor nodded and said, this indicates the radiance
penetrated to your internal organs. What happened next?
I told him – I looked directly into the man's eyes. In his
eyes, there was my reflection, and it was tiny and twisted.
What sensations were experienced at this point, the
inquisitor asked.
I told him: I felt tiny and twisted.
The inquisitor nodded.
What happened next, he asked.
I told him – the curtains closed, and the man disappeared.
And though the window was dark again, I couldn't see my
reflection in the glass any more.
And then I fell onto the pavement, and I found I was crying.
The inquisitor nodded again. Yes, he said. Loss of moral
control. That is the next stage of the radiance sickness.

Tara   In my hand is the bread knife.
I've run out of the house, down the alley and through the
streets and I'm still carrying this bread knife.

Beat.

I stop running.

It takes Julian a few seconds to sense I've fallen behind.
He turns, slowing but not quite coming to a halt.
Their footsteps are close, and he doesn't dare shout at me to
come on, to catch up with him.
He stares, and his stare pleads.

Kelly   The inquisitor puts his arm round me.
I pull back, but he holds me there.
He says – you understand now, don't you.
You understand how dangerous they are.
You understand now why all sources of radiance have to be
removed.
He holds my gaze. I nod.
He smiles at me.
I hand over my pistol.

Tara   Julian.
Julian.
Sometimes, when we're together.
We're together in bed.
I cry out or clutch you the wrong way and you stop, you
pull back, you wipe the sweat from my forehead and you
search my face and I can see you thinking – have I hurt her?
Have I?
And you never have hurt me, you almost never have and
even if you have, a little, that look, that care, that tenderness
melts whatever tiny hurt there might have been, and I want
to pull you down as hard as I can into me.
Think about that.
Think how careful you are with me.
When they catch us, it'll be the exact opposite.
Not your gentle fingers teasing me open, but their ragged
nails forcing a way in. Not your kisses, but their curses and
spit.

Julian   They might not catch us.

Tara   Not your face, but a half-dozen of theirs, peering
down their snouts at me, wondering 'Have we hurt her?
Have we hurt her yet?'

Julian   I won't let them / [touch you]

Tara   / Two of them hold you, while the other ten beat you senseless. Once you're broken on the floor, they'll turn their attention to me. They'll prop bits of you up so you can admire their technique. You'll close your eyes, so they'll spare a moment to snip off your eyelids.
But. Now there's just us. And –
– I've got this knife.

Julian *looks*.

Tara   They'll take us apart.
And then they'll be able to put us back together, any way they want.

Kelly   I'm shaking again.
What is it, the inquisitor asks. You may as well just say.
I tell him –
– those eyes.
I want them.
I want them to be mine.

Tara   We've got this moment.
We have this opportunity
To put ourselves out of harm's way.
Now: quickly.
Before they find us, and make us less than we are.

Julian   Everything you're saying seems to add up
But I don't see how it can.
You're right, but I don't see how you can be.

Tara (*beat*)   I put my arm, my left arm, round his neck.
I pull him close.
The point slides in an inch and then bounces back like a spade hitting rock –
– he staggers, falls forward, falls to his knees and I hold him up and now I can lean in, use my weight to drive the point deeper, and as the knife's teeth scrape against bone, I pull him tight, I catch his eyes –

Julian   You're right.

But I can't do what needs to be done.
I can't understand how anyone could.

Darren   I've not left the house since. I've not.
I've sat, and I've waited for the knock on the door.
And –
– it's not a knock, it's . . . a thump.
I count to five and I – look through the peephole and –
She's staring right at me.
I throw back the bolts and the chains and I open the door –
– he stumbles onto me.
I catch him –
– there's this handle sticking out of him, and I grab it and
pull and it's a knife, it was so far in him I couldn't even see
the blade, and now there's all this blood –
– he's too heavy so I let him slide down to the floor –
– she's standing at the doorway, looking at me.

Kelly   His eyes.
I want them.
I want them to be mine.

Darren   There are sirens and boots crunching along the
street.
I've got no voice.
I don't need a voice.
Because: she knows.
She steps over the threshold.
She turns the locks and slides the bolts.
She's come.

Kelly   I want those eyes to be mine, I tell him.
You can have them, he says.
You can have them for your very own.
You just have to find them.

Scene Two

Darren   When I still went to work.
When I could still get on the train and bear those carefully
frozen faces.
When I could still bear to leave the house and go to work,
my last project at the ministry involved cataloguing certain
sound recordings.
The recordings were made by putting a subject into a
carefully miked room, and tying the subject to a chair. And
then forcing a hose down the subject's throat. And then
putting a funnel in the top of the hose. And then pouring
bleach into the funnel.
The recordings were created for morale purposes: they
would be broadcast over the far-speaker network to stiffen
the resolve of the citizenry, in the event of a collapse of
national moral will.
The subjects involved in these recordings were citizens who
had tried to help non-citizens evade quarantine orders.

Beat.

I have listened to these recordings at length, over the course
of the project. And yet I wasn't worried when the police
came round conducting routine door-to-door. I wasn't
worried about their counters clicking away, measuring
ambient radiance. I wasn't worried about the bloodstains on
the floor. Because everything was going to plan, and the
plan did not include the police dragging me off to the dark
rooms under the ministry.
If anything, it was the bloke that was worrying me. 'Cause I
didn't know what he was *for*.
But he didn't worry me too much: because he was obviously
going to die.

Tara   When the police came we hid in the cellar. Julian
was still drifting in and out of consciousness and I –
I didn't think this guy was going to say anything. I can
imagine life takes a sudden, dark turn for citizens who get
caught sheltering our sort.

It was just: what if they come in. What if they search the place. What if they see all the blood on the hall floor –
And Julian was still drifting.
I was on my own.

Darren   After the police went, I left a discreet pause. I didn't want to bother her immediately.
Not after what had clearly been a stressful morning.
(*To* **Tara**.) What do you want to do?
I'd suggest we go to a café, but that's not really on
What with the curfew, and the cops looking for you, and everything.
But we could have a drink here.

Tara   I'm sorry?

Darren (*beat*)   I've got tea.
I've got water, not sparkling but bottled at least.
You can't trust the taps these days, can you.

Waits for a response from **Tara***: none comes.*

Perhaps you're in the mood for something stronger.
It's my habit to take a reviving draught of German lager at about this time of day.
Obviously I can't get German lager. Not since the borders closed.
There are varieties of home-produced which are fairly crisp and fresh.
But usually you can't get them either. Not legally.
I have, however, extensive supplies of clear spirit they sell in five-litre plastic flagons. I bought it in bulk, before they brought in the rationing. I had a little warning, you see: contacts at the ministry.

Waits for a response from **Tara***: none comes.*

I expect you're going to tell me I shouldn't be touching that rubbish.
Aren't you.
You're going to tell me I don't need that crap in my system.
Well.

I'm sure you'll wean me off it soon enough.

Tara   What the hell are you talking about?

Darren   Just saying now you're around I won't be
needing to hit the bottle quite so much, will I.
I say bottle, I mean, of course, five-litre plastic flagon.

Tara (*stares at him*)   Jesus Christ.

Beat.

Darren   So . . . do you want some tea?

Tara   No, thank you.

Darren   Or some –
– or some stovecakes?
I've got some stovecakes left, I could heat them up for you /

Tara   / Will you just – leave me alone? Please?

Beat.

Darren (*to* **Tara**)   You could be a bit more –

Tara's *look cuts him off.*

You don't have to take it out on me.
It's not my fault, all this.
I've just tried to *help*.

Beat.

Tara   I've heard.
I've heard these rumours about factories.
Rendering factories where they send the corpses of diseased
animals and rip out their spines and brains and hearts, so
the disease can be contained.
The rumours say – our kind end up in these factories.
What the rumours don't say.
What I don't understand is –
– which part of us do you think is diseased? Our brains?
Our hearts? Our nerves, what?

Darren   None of those.

Kelly   None of that.

Tara   What is it about me that's diseased?

Darren   These factories –

Kelly   It's your skin.

Darren   – I used to work at the ministry.

Kelly   Your smile.

Darren   I worked keeping records.

Kelly   Your *eyes*.

Darren   These factories – are staffed by volunteers. It used to be that the volunteers were just blinded.
But then a volunteer traced his fingers over the body of one of your kind.
And just by feeling the contours of her dead skin, the radiance entered him.
He broke down, abandoned his rendering machine, and had to be shot.
Now, the volunteers' hands are bathed in acid at the end of every week, so their fingers are always scabbed and bleeding. And unfeeling.
Before the factories, undertakers, coroners, morgue technicians – dozens of them were afflicted with radiance sickness while handling your kind. This led to acute moral weakness. There were tears and mood swings. They found themselves paralysed by sunsets and birdsong. Ultimately, it led to dissidence. And being shot by the secret police.
But with blinded eyes and burned hands and rendering machines, you can be disposed of safely.
Referendum day.
I wanted to vote and say they should leave you alone.
But I couldn't –
– find a way to leave the house.
Because out on the streets.

Beat.

It was bad enough when they let your lot walk around the

place. Mid-conversation one of you'd swan past and –
– everything stopped for a few seconds.
We'd pull ourselves together and struggle to pick back up
whatever we were talking about before the sparkle in your
eyes or bounce in your hair made whatever we were talking
about seem small, ridiculous, laughable . . .
Then when they got you off the streets . . .
Without you there was just us.

Beat.

Our –

Kelly   – oozing skin. Our ruined teeth.

Darren   Talking about whatever small, ridiculous,
laughable things we had to talk about. With no hope that
one of you might walk past and /
/ I couldn't bear it.
Those *faces.*

Beat.

She can't even look at me.
She can't meet my eyes
Her gaze slides right off me.
How can she save me if she can't even look at me?

Kelly   She can't save you, obviously.

Tara   We'd never do this to you.
We'd try to help, if there was a problem.
We'd never exterminate your kind, just to save ourselves.
We'd rather die.

Beat.

Darren   How is he?
Your friend.

Tara (*looks at* **Darren**)   He's fine.

Turns away from him.

He's fine except he can't speak.

His eyes flick open occasionally but they don't focus
properly: they focus on empty points in the room. Like he's
seeing into another world. Like he's leaving me already.

Beat.

And I don't know what to do.
We had plans.
He told me a story about the day that involved cutting back
the rhododendrons and pruning the roses. It didn't involve –
Any of this.
And he's asleep.
He's left me alone.
I hug him and his breath
Sets the hairs of my neck on end
He's wrapped in blankets
Blankets this citizen gave us
He smells of them
He smells like a citizen
I pull them off and bury my head in his chest
I open his shirt so I can taste his skin: and it tastes of blood
I open my eyes and I can see into the cut
I can see
I can see his heart.
The cold of the basement
is freezing it.
I can see ice crystals
Forming inside the cut.
He is freezing from the inside out.

Darren   It's this bloke.

Tara   If he woke he could tell me what we should do with
the rest of the day.
But if he woke, and he was frozen from the inside
– he might not be able to speak.
He might be less than he was.

Darren   It's 'cause this bloke's still here.
That's what's fucking things up.

Tara   He agreed with me it was best that we just –

– take care of ourselves before they could get to us.

Darren   He's supposed to get her here, to me, and then –
– he dies, right?
I sit with him. I watch him breathing.
Really shallow breathing.
He could go any moment, the blood he's lost.
I could wait for that moment.
Or I could pick up a pillow.

Tara   He'd given his consent.

Darren   Push it over his face.

Tara   And they did come, the police did come for us.

Darren   He's barely conscious anyway.

Tara   He'd promised they wouldn't, but they did.

Darren   Or if he is conscious, he must be in dreadful pain.

Tara   He agreed it was for the best.

Julian *looks at her.*

Tara (*meets his gaze; looks away; to* **Darren**)   You know what you can do.
If you want to do something for us.

Darren   What? What d'you need?

Tara   We can't get away.
He's too –
– Julian's too weak to move.

Darren   I know; perhaps some sweet tea, or I have a little broth /

Tara   / I don't think broth is going to be enough to make him better. I think he's going to die.

Darren (*beat*)   I think you're very brave to face up to that.

Tara   Rather than waiting and running the risk that the police will find us and do God knows what I'm going to end it.

Darren *looks.*

Tara   And when I've done that.
If you want to make up.
If you want to make up for all the things your people have done to us.
I've got this knife.
I want to go with him.
I won't know what to do unless he's there to –
I don't want to wake up and know the world hates me.

Beat.

If I can't finish the job.
Will you do it for me?

Darren *looks.*

Tara   If you don't want to use the knife, you could use a pillow or something, you could just put it over my head. Please.

Darren   I can't.

Tara   You really have to.

Julian   I wake up and the first thought that forms in my mind is: did Tara have time to kill herself before they got to her?

Tara   Honey.

Julian   I woke up and I was alone.

Tara   I was here, sweetheart. I haven't left you.

Julian   But I woke up and it was dark and I was alone.

Tara   You must've –
– that must've been a dream, sweetheart. If you wake up and I'm not here – that's just a dream. I'd never leave you alone.

Julian   I remember: turning away from her.
The strength draining from my legs.
Falling into a door: and then the door collapsing under my weight.
Not collapsing. Opening. The door opened.
This – citizen – let us in.

Tara   Yes he did.

Julian   I look at him. He has –
– the look of all good citizens: damp, waxy skin, a bed for mosses and fungus. Fingers as rough and stubby as twigs.
And eyes –
(*To* **Darren**.) What's your name?

Darren   I'm called Darren.

Julian   In his eyes –
(*To* **Darren**.) – why did you help us?

Darren (*looks*)   I even want to tell him.
I want to be honest with him now, in his last moments.
I want to thank him for bringing her to me.
I want to tell him: I let you in because I had no choice. I was going to die if she hadn't come to save me. And I really don't want to die.

Julian   He stutters and flails for words.
(*To* **Darren**.) It's okay. I understand. You let us in because you had to.

Darren *looks at him.*

Julian   You had to because you don't want to die.

Darren *nods.*

Julian   Soon enough, they'll have killed every last one of us.
Rendered our bodies. Buried the evidence at sea.
Then the ministry will start work on your people. They'll get rid of anyone who carries a remnant, an echo of our kind.
The boy whose eyes have a half-pleasing symmetry – when closed, so you can't see the sixty-degree laziness. The girl

with nice legs, if a catastrophic face.
Each one of you who is touched by the ghost of us – filtered out.
And that's how you'll die.
The ministry will blame it on agents introduced into the water supply by hostile Western powers.
Or sunspot activity.
Or an unfavourable alignment of the planets.
But you'll know the truth.
Won't you.

Darren *looks at him.*

Julian   You won't be able to stand the sight of each other.
First, it'll be babies abandoned on the streets because mothers can't bear to look at them.
Then no babies at all, because you can't bear to come near one another.
And then those of you who are left will wither and die
For the want of one moment of warmth.
For the want of a smile.

Beat.

You can feel it coming, can't you?
You can feel all that coming for you.
(*To* **Tara**.) I was an idiot.
I thought: if you fight, if you resist, if you give them something to overcome, some act of struggle they can focus on to distract themselves from the act of killing: that they can manage. But if you just stand there and let them.
They have to look you in the eye as they open your throat.
I thought they wouldn't be able to. Well, maybe the soldiers could, they're caught up in the action, the busyness of it all but: perhaps the officer, I thought.
The officer, standing back, supervising, overseeing, with time to reflect on what she was doing. I thought she might have qualms.
But obviously no. The officer has her orders. Clearly printed. Formulated entirely in declarative sentences, for the

avoidance of qualms and scruples and all kinds of doubt.
I should have known it would be an ordinary citizen.
An ordinary citizen who looked out of his window, and saw
us and simply couldn't let us die.
Because he understood we're all the same.

Darren   But – we're not.
I'm not the same as you.

Julian   If they find us here, what will happen to you?

Kelly   A visit to a carefully miked-up room.
A funnel, a hose shoved down the throat.

Julian   You sheltered us to save yourself; I know that. But
it doesn't matter.
You sheltered us: you put yourself in our shoes.

Darren   She can't meet my eyes.
Her gaze slides right off me.
Because I'm.
Because I am the way I am, and no more.

Julian   When you sheltered us, you joined us.
You made yourself the same as us.

Darren   No, you don't –
I don't think you understand.

Julian   I do understand.
Whyever you think you sheltered us.
Whatever you think the reason was.
It doesn't matter.

Darren (*beat*)   He tries to reach up to me from the bed.
The rags bandaging his chest are brown with stale blood.
From the wound itself, a sweet sharp smell.
It's a smell –
– that reminds me of walking in a forest.
Dappled green light. Seven years old. With a girl – her
name was –
– not important.
Pushing through brambles, we came to a clearing and

suddenly the air was heavy and sweet.
She bent down, as if she was going to pick a flower.
And held up the skull by one of its horns. She held it up for
me to see – and the whole thing came apart.
The horn came apart from the skull, and the skull fell to the
floor and cracked open, and the brain popped out: except it
wasn't the brain, it was a ball of maggots and flies that
dissolved into the air around us.
We both ran out of the forest and into the fields and she
cried and cried and I thought she'd never stop.

Beat: he looks to **Tara**.

And that was my first ever kiss.

Beat.

He hugs me, and reaches out to the woman, and pulls her
close, pulls her arms around him, and so pulls her arms
around me.
I can feel the warmth of her against my back.

Beat.

(*To* **Julian**.) We're going to need food, then.
If you're going to stay.

Julian   Of course we're going to stay. Because this is how
it begins. This is how the change comes. From the three of
us.

Darren   My rations won't be enough.
But there are people you can go to, if you've got stuff to sell.

Tara   Have you got anything we can sell?

Darren   No.
But you have.

Scene Three

Kelly   The inquisitor said:
We are close to a generalised solution to the problem of the
non-citizenry. At this time, however, ground actions are still
useful.
It is in this aspect that we propose to deploy you.
I had been instructed to remove my uniform.
I stood, naked.
The inquisitor looked away. Obviously.
An under-secretary arrived with civilian clothes. Averting
his eyes, he placed them on the floor next to me.
You will dress, and go out into the city.
What will I do to be of service to the ministry, I asked.
There are collaborators, the inquisitor told me, who shelter
non-citizens. Inevitably, they become infected with traces of
radiance. The very susceptibility that left you unable to
carry out this quarantine order makes you useful in tracking
these collaborators.
Your moral weakness, your vulnerability to infection, your
sensitivity to radiance, will lead you to them.

Beat.

They let me go.

Darren *seems to hear her.*

Kelly   They set me loose.

Darren *is aware of her voice.*

Kelly   I found myself down by the harbour.
I found him.

Beat.

He . . . presented himself to me.

Daren *looks at her.*

Kelly (*look back at him*)   He made a gift of himself to me.
(*To* **Darren**.) Hello.

Darren   Hi. (*He looks away.*)

Kelly   I imagined I would feel some – trepidation.
But then I looked at him.
At his –
– skin hair throat *eyes* –
– and it was fine.
I wanted him –
– taken away.
Removed from my sight.
I mean –

Darren   No –

Kelly   I mean –
Fine.

Darren   No. This has to be –
All that time searching.
Then realising that searching was wrong
That waiting was right;
All that time hidden behind those doors
And then she comes
And she doesn't come alone –
– she's there now in my house.
And she's not alone.
And I'm out here.
On the streets again.
With all this –

Kelly   There was –

Darren   – all this ugliness –

Kelly   – something – a sulk, carved into his cheek,
Something that brought down the tone of the planet,
Something that made it so much easier.
Something –

Beat.

That reminded me of myself.
(*She looks at* **Darren**.) Hello

Darren   Hi.

Kelly   You fucking – filthy fucking –
– are you really going to make this
So fucking easy for me you fucking –
(*She catches herself; smiles at* **Darren**.)
I give the nod to the plainclothes butchers
Who've been assigned to me.
(*Looks at him.*)
Have you got . . .

Darren *looks at her.*

Kelly (*holds his gaze; then*)   Have you got something . . . to
sell?

Darren *looks away.*

Kelly   Because I'm looking to buy.
If you've got anything.
Whatever you might have, I'm in that market.

Darren   I've got some . . . stuff.

Kelly   Hand it over, then.

Beat.

Don't get all tense.
Don't look at me.
Don't pretend not to be doing anything.
Just sit there, look at the sea, look at the sea gulls, and then
when you're ready, without warning, without any great big
fuss, take the package from under your jacket and give it to
me. (*Looks at him.*)

Darren *looks at her.*

Kelly   What?

Darren   Don't you want to –
– check out . . . the merchandise?

Kelly *looks at him.*

Darren   I'm sorry if that's really naïve.

I've never done this before –

Kelly   – yes I do.
Yes of course I want to.

Beat.

Go ahead then.

Darren   Out here?
In the open?
You want me to –
– show you the stuff?
In the open? Where people will see?

Kelly   The butchers are closing in.
Reaching under their regulation trenchcoats
For their regulation skin-shavers
Their regulation finger-snippers
Their regulation eye-hooks.
(*Beat. To* **Darren**.) We'll go –
We'll get some privacy.

Beat.

I give another nod to the butchers.
This nod says: just, back off.
Just, keep your distance.
Don't scare the little baby away.

Darren   She leads me up an alley.

Kelly   Let's have a look then.

Darren *looks at her.*

Kelly   He was nervous –
– but there was something else as well.

Beat.

I went to take the package from him and his grip tightened
round it.
He didn't want to let it go.

Darren   You –

– don't look with your hands.

Kelly (*looks at him; smiles*)   No you don't.
And he reached in to the package.
And pulled out –

Beat.

– oh my God . . .

Darren   I watched Julian gather her hair in his hand, like
he was going to make a ponytail.
I said, when he went to sharpen the blade, I told him he was
getting it wrong.
He said –

Julian   I know what I'm doing, trust me.

Darren   But I really think, the way you're doing it, I think
that makes the blade even duller –

Julian   – I think what's important is that we get this over
with as quickly as possible. I think what's important is that
we minimise the trauma of the experience for Tara.

Darren (*goes to reply to him: chickens out*)   The edge was still
dull when he started to cut.
He had to drag the knife through her hair like it was straw.
He hurt her.
It's not straw.
It's fine and soft and –

Kelly   – it picks up the sun, it spins and the sun sparkles
off it

Darren   – and he hurt her.

Kelly   Bursts of silver light up the alleyway
Drain pipes and dustbin lids gleam and –
– oh . . .

Darren (*to* **Kelly**)   The money, please.

Kelly *looks at him.*

Darren   Can I have the money, please.

Kelly   Let me see it again.

Darren   You can.
You see it.
And – touch it.

Kelly *groans.*

Darren   And smell it.
And have it for your very own.
As soon as you hand over the money.

Beat.

Kelly   Where did you get that?

Darren *doesn't answer.*

Kelly   That looked . . . fresh.
She can't have been long dead
When you harvested that.

Darren   She wasn't –

Kelly   – wasn't . . . long dead.

Darren   No.

Kelly   Wasn't . . . dead at all?

Darren *can't answer.*

Kelly   He steps away from me.

Darren   If you don't want the stuff, that's just fine.

Kelly   Oh I want it.

Darren   It's fine, I'll sell it somewhere else.

Kelly   And he –
– he's backing away and
He rubs his hand over his mouth
The hand that'd held her hair
And his mouth –

Darren   What?

Kelly   – his lips.

Darren   What are you –
– looking at?

Kelly   A sheen of light over his lips.

Darren   What are you – doing?

Kelly   A sheen of – radiance
Over his lips.
I step closer.

Darren   No.

Kelly   I close my eyes.

Darren   No.

Kelly   I have to because
His cheeks, his nose, his eyes
These are all unaffected.
But his lips.

Darren   Don't you –

Kelly   His lips.

Darren   Please.

Kelly   His mouth.

Darren   Oh God, no . . .

Kelly   I keep that in my mind
That image in my mind.
The shine.
The radiance.

Darren   Don't – touch me…

Kelly   The radiance on his lips touches mine
And my eyes are closed and I can barely remember his
throat and hair and skin.
And – it's in me.

Darren   What have you done . . .

Kelly   I swallow it down.

Darren   What have you done to me?

Kelly   It's in me.

Darren *looks at her.*

Kelly (*beat; she smiles*)   The butchers . . .
Have been getting all worked up.
They've been stroking their blades under their trenchcoats.
You can see the cuts in their fingertips
You can see the pits in the leather of their fingers.
These cuts are inches deep, and they never bleed.
The master butcher says:
Where'd he go? Where's the target?
I tell him: false alarm.
So fuck off.
Fuck off and let me do my job.

Beat.

As our lips parted,
I prised open my eyelids.
I managed to look at him
Even as our bodies touched.
We looked
And we touched
And not even one of us then needed to die.

Scene Four

Julian   You're back.

Darren   I am.

Julian *looks at him.*

Darren   What?

Julian   I don't know.
There's –
– did it go well?

Darren   I suppose.
How are you?

Julian   I'm… well. I suppose. (*Looks at him.*)

Beat.

Darren   What?

Julian   I don't know.
I think you've caught the sun.

Darren (*looks at him*)   I –
– haven't been out for a while.
So that could happen quite quickly, I suppose.

Julian   Looks good on you, a little bit of colour.

Darren (*looks at him; then*)   Do you want to eat, then?

Kelly   When I get home, I go up into the loft.
Hidden away, under tea chests and mouldy clothes
I find a relic.
A framed advertisement for a Western cola drink.
This advertisement is printed on a mirror.

Julian   I'm starving.

Darren   And what about Tara?

Tara   I'm fine.

Beat.

Julian   She's fine, apparently.

Kelly   I prop the mirror on the mantelpiece.
I open the bag.
I pull out –
– I take it out.
I want to open the curtains so it will catch the light but
Of course I don't risk letting anyone see.

Julian   You should eat something.

Tara *doesn't answer.*

Julian   A few mouthfuls to keep your strength up.

Tara   As if you –

Julian   Please.

Beat.

Tara   Thank you.

Darren   You're . . . very welcome.

Kelly   I hold the hair up by my –
– I rub it over my face.
I breathe in its smell.
I tuck it behind my ears.
I lay it over my head.
I drape it in a fringe before my eyes.
I look in the mirror.
I look –
– ridiculous.
I look – (*She dries up.*)

Darren   This won't last forever, of course.

Julian   No.

Darren   We'll need more money.

Kelly   I look –

Beat.

I need more.

Beat.

Julian   Yes of course. (*He looks to* **Tara**.)

Tara *ignores him.*

Julian   Tara.

Beat.

Tara will you fetch me the knife.

Beat.

Tara will you fetch me the knife, please.

Darren (*quietly*)   No.

Julian   Tara will you fetch me the knife and the whetstone. Please.

Darren   No.
No, you don't –
You're too weak.
You should rest.

Julian *looks at him.*

Darren (*beat; then*)   As I draw the knife against the whetstone, she shivers
I want to say: no. Don't –
– there's no need to be afraid.
I'm doing it right.
I'm making the blade sharper.
I'm making it easier.
I don't say that.
I just draw the blade against the stone.
I let her shiver.

Beat.

I gather her hair –
I touch her hair.
I touch her.
And she shivers.
I want to say, no, don't shiver,
I'm not –
– I'm doing this so we can be together–
– so we can live. So we can eat.

Beat.

Her hair is already cropped close by now
So I have to
Grip it quite tightly.
I have to
Bring the blade very close to her skin

And in doing this my knuckles brush against
Her scalp, the nape of her neck, her earlobes.

Beat.

And she shivers.
I want to say,
Please don't shiver at my touch.
Please don't –
– don't shiver like that.

Kelly   Hello again.

Darren *looks at her.*

Kelly   Didn't expect to see you back so soon.

Darren *says nothing.*

Kelly   I mean I hoped to.

Beat.

Darren   I've got more stuff.

Beat.

Kelly   Okay.

Beat.

He lifts the bag towards me.
And his hands –
– his hands are gleaming.
I think those hands could touch me.
And neither of us would need to die.

Darren   Do you want it, then?

Beat.

Kelly   Yes. Please.

Darren   I'll need –
– the price has gone up, this time.

Kelly   That's fine.

Beat.

Darren   Good.

Kelly *looks at him.*

Darren   Well then.

Kelly   You know /

Darren *looks at her.*

Kelly   You're putting yourself in an awful lot of danger.

Darren *looks at her.*

Kelly   It's an awful lot of danger just – for money.

(*She looks at him.*)

It's not just for money, is it.
They're still alive.
You're sheltering them.
You're protecting them.

Darren *looks at her.*

Kelly   Why?

Darren   You wouldn't understand.

Beat.

Kelly   It's because you're going to die for want of a kiss
Or a smile
Or a touch

Beat. She reaches for him.

Darren   Don't.

Kelly (*pulls back*)   You could turn them in.
There are ways to turn them in
Without being . . . implicated.
I could help you. I have connections.

Darren   No.

Kelly   I kissed you.

Darren   No.

Kelly   And you didn't –

Darren   No.

Beat.

Kelly   We could –

Darren (*looks at her*)   From her pocket, she pulls a lock of
Tara's hair
She rubs it over her mouth . . . and –

Kelly   You see?
Do you see?
Just – step closer.
Just close your eyes.
Just don't think of me.
I don't mind
If you think of her.
You have to think of her.
But it'll be me.
And we can be together.
We can use what we have of them
To be together
And make it bearable
And neither of us will need to die.

Beat.

There.
You see?

Darren *looks at her.*

Kelly   You see?

Beat. She smiles.

Darren *looks at her.*

Kelly   No. Don't . . .

Darren   / How do you know I can't have her?

Kelly   Oh God, don't . . .

Darren   / How do you know I can't have her properly? How do you know she couldn't ever want me?

Kelly   Because . . . (*Stares at him.*)

Darren *gradually, gradually drops his gaze to the floor.*

Scene Five

Darren *looks at* **Julian**.

Julian   You were dreaming.

Darren   Yeah?

Julian   I was too.

Darren   You were too?

Julian (*nods*)   I think you were having a nice dream. Weren't you?

Darren *doesn't answer.*
What were you dreaming of?

Darren (*beat*)   I – can't tell you.

Darren   What were you dreaming about?

Julian   Our glorious future. When we've triumphed over the forces of darkness and returned the nation to sanity. And we live together in peace. Brothers in the struggle . . .

Darren *laughs with him.*

Julian   Don't you fucking . . . giggle at my dreams.

Darren   I'm not laughing at your dreams, mate, just your –
I mean, 'brothers in the struggle'.

Julian (*smiles*)   Well: we are, aren't we.

Darren   Of course.

Beat.

Julian   But what?

Darren (*looks at him*)   Is Tara awake?

Julian *shakes his head.*

Darren   She –
She never looks at me.
She can never bring herself to look at me.

Beat.

Julian   Well, she – (*Looks at him.*)
She's afraid.

Darren   She's afraid of me?

Julian   It's not you: it's all the people you remind her of.
The soldiers. The ministry officials. The police.
Obviously you have the same . . . look.
It touches a nerve.

Darren   What kind of look?

Julian   I don't know, nothing in particular –

Darren   – tell me because if it's something I could change
I would if that would make things easier for Tara –

Julian   It's nothing, it's just –
I don't know.
It's nothing.

Beat.

It's nothing to do with you.
It's to do with other people.
We don't think about you –
– you're not like them.
You're like us.
You, me, Tara: we're the same.

Darren   I don't know if we are the same.
You know what to think, and what to do.

I get confused.
Sometimes I think – (*He looks at* **Julian**.)
– sometimes I see a cop in the street and I think I could just
walk up to her and tell her all about you.
They'd come and take you away and I could throw myself
on the mercy of the state. They'd probably kill me but –

Beat.

Julian   – if you were dead, you wouldn't be scared shitless
any more.

Darren *nods.*

Beat.

Julian   You reckon I don't think about just running into
the street? Letting them tear me to pieces?

Darren   I don't believe you.

Julian   Well: do. It's the truth.
The temptation to just end things
It's there all the time.
But I know I won't give in to it.
And I know you won't.

Darren *looks at him. Senses* **Tara** *– leaves.*

Tara (*watches* **Darren** *retreat*)   He's going to crack.

Julian   He is not.

Beat.

Tara   Do you really get tempted?
To give in.
Do you?

Julian *looks at her.*

Tara   Of course you don't.

Julian   I told him what he needed to hear.

Tara   No, it's not that. I don't give a fuck what you tell
him.

It's – as if you could ever have a moment of doubt.

Julian *looks at her.*

Tara   We should try and make it to the border.

Julian   I'm not well enough to travel.

Tara   You're not going to get any better here.

Beat.

He'd go with us. I bet he would.
He could be our cover. He could do the talking.

Julian   Do you really think so?

Tara (*beat*)   It's our best chance to get out of here alive.

Julian   Perhaps it is.

Tara (*beat*)   But you don't want to get out of here.

Julian   If they kill us all –

Tara   Serve them fucking right.

Julian   We're not worth more than the citizens.
Or do you disagree?
Do you think we are better than them?

Tara   No, obviously not.

Julian   They can all go to hell, so long as we two are saved?

Tara (*looks at him*)   Well: yeah, I think I'm better than them now.
I'm better than them because of what they've done.
I'm better than them because – I've never killed anybody.

Beat.

Why should it be me that has to stay here and at any moment they could come through the door and take us off and –

Beat.

If they come, it'll be me that has to live through it while they do things to my body. It'll be me.

Beat.

Don't you want to save me?

Julian   You know when I understood it would take the world?

Beat.

Because it makes no sense. The world doesn't want to kill itself. We don't all want to die.
I don't think we even really want to kill.
But we want to know what it's like.
We want to know what it's like, to press a button that launches a bomb.
We want to know what it's like to pull a trigger.
We want to know quite how a person screams when their skin catches fire.
We want to know –
– we're just curious as to how much resistance there is when you push a knife into someone.
We wonder how that resistance changes as the point of the blade slips past the layers of skin and flesh and into the cavity of the chest.
We wonder, inevitably, about the look that passes over a person's face when the blade touches them in places they've never been touched before.

Beat.

No, you've never killed anybody.
You didn't quite manage it, did you.

Tara *looks.*

Julian   We want to know how these catastrophes feel.
And when an excuse presents itself.

Tara *says nothing.*

Julian   What divides us is

How we behave
When an excuse presents itself.

Beat.

Tara   If we're staying, we'll need more money for food.

Julian   We will.

Beat.

Tara   We'll have to find something else to sell.

Beat.

Darren   I came awake from a dream where Tara was
screaming –
– I sat shivering, waiting for my head to clear –
– and Tara screamed again.
(*To* **Julian**.) What's going on?

Julian *says nothing.*

Darren   What the fuck's going on?
Where's Tara?

Julian   She's in the bathroom.
She's fine.

Darren   What the fuck's been going on?

Beat.

His face is guiltless. Serene and unlined
as he open his hand –

Beat.

Seven years old.
This ram's skull exploding
And amidst the flies and shrapnel
Its teeth.
Much longer than you'd think.
They've got roots, sunk deep into the jaw.
So deep that if you try to pull them out you're almost bound
to crack the bone.

Beat.

– and he tips it out onto the table and raises the pliers –

Julian   I'll just smash the tooth so we can get to the
filling –

Darren   *No* –

Beat.

– no, don't do that.
They – prefer it.
You get a higher price for the gold if the filling is still in the
tooth.
So they can be sure where it came from.
And what someone went through to give it up. (*He starts.*)

Tara   Sorry.

Beat.

Darren   Her mouth was like
When a child gets hold of lipstick and paints it round and
round out from her mouth till her mouth takes over most of
her face.
She was pressing this rag to her jaw: when she took the rag
away blood bubbled up and filled her mouth.
On her jaw, I thought I could see –
There were what looked like.
He must have had to hold her jaw steady.
And there were these . . . indentations.
From where he must have put his boot.

Beat.

I saw all this.
I could see all that detail because
She looked at me.
She stared straight at me.
She let me look at her.
And she didn't mind.

Tara   Sorry about the noise.

Darren   And of course the surface matters
But that's okay.
That's okay now because
She has this ruined mouth
And now she will look at me
And although the surface affects the inside
If you were to hold your hand over that ruined mouth
You'd hardly be able to tell, from looking in her eyes
You'd hardly notice at all.

Tara   I'm sorry if we woke you up.

Darren   That's fine. It's no problem.
It's about time I was up anyway.
You know: taking actions. Doing things.
So that's really just fine.

Scene Six

Kelly   Hiya.

Darren   Hello.

Kelly (*beat*)   Were you looking for me?

He doesn't answer.

Have you got something to sell?

Darren   No.

Kelly (*looks at him*)   Yes you have.
Yes you have, I can / smell it

Darren   I don't want to deal with you anymore.

Kelly (*beat*)   Perhaps you don't.
Tough bloody luck.
Let me see.

Kelly *looks at her.*

Kelly   Oh my Christ.
It's . . . beautiful.

And there's still –
– there's still blood on it.
(*Looks at him.*) It's still alive.
We could knock one of my teeth out
And plant hers in the hole
Maybe it would take root in my jaw.
It would grow in me.
And then –
we could . . .

Darren *says nothing.*

Kelly   I know . . . you don't want to be alone.
You don't have to be.
If you could just . . .
. . . close your eyes and –

Darren   No.

Kelly *looks at him.*

Darren   No.

Kelly   You have to.

Darren   No.

Kelly   I'm your own kind.

Darren *looks at her.*

Kelly   We have to try.

Darren   I'd rather –

Beat.

How can we be together
When we know –

Kelly   What?

Darren   Look at me.
Go on. Look.
Look at it all.
Cast of skin and stink of mouth

And fear and shame and fear in the eyes.
How could you –
We could be together?
How could you be – with this
When you know – *they exist.*

Kelly   I could – close my eyes.
I could use my imagination.
I could – learn to bear it.
I could.
I think I really could.

Beat.

Do you think you could?

He doesn't answer.

Do you think you might?

He doesn't answer.

Do you –

She looks at him. She looks away.

Darren (*beat*)   I think
I'd better deal with someone else from now on.

Kelly (*struggles; recovers herself*)   Darren.
Before you go.
There's just one thing.

Darren *looks at her.*

Kelly   You're under arrest.

Darren *comes to a stop.*

Kelly   Don't look so shocked.
You knew who I was the second you set eyes on me.

Beat.

You knew I was coming for you.

Beat.

Who am I?

Darren   The police?

Kelly   I'm an angel.
I'm the angel come to save you.

Darren   I'm going to have to go now.

Kelly   You take one step and I'll shoot you . . .
. . . in the throat?
How'd you feel about that?

Darren   Not good.

Kelly   No.
Messy. Painful. Can take a while. Or it can be instant if the
bullet severs the spinal cord.
Now. Obviously I'm not a real angel, because real angels
don't go threatening to shoot people in the throat. Or at
least they shouldn't do.
But I might be your angel.
Your guardian angel.

Beat.

I'm here to save your life.

Beat.

How this works is.
What you have to understand is –
– they're dead now.
These –

Darren   – people –

Kelly   – that you're sheltering.
They're dead.
Nothing you can do will change that.

She waits for a moment.

Now, given that they're dead, all that's left is you.
Your future.
And you might still have a future.

Traditionally, what you've done gets you a trip to a room
with an earth-packed floor.
The earth soaks up blood and other bodily fluids,
apparently.
But you might still be redeemed.
Because we need them alive.
There are tests. There is an effort towards a generalised
solution to the problem of the non-citizenry. This effort
would be enhanced by the availability of live specimens.
Now I know I've just told you they're dead.
But the fact is, they're not. Just yet. But it helps – it will help
you walk the particular road down which I want to
encourage you – if you think of them as being dead. Which
they effectively are. Despite being factually alive.
You could run now. You might get away from me. You
might get to them and give them a warning. And they'd –
kill themselves, probably. That's what usually happens.
So they'll be dead. And shortly after that, so will you be.
Or you can lead us to them.
We can take them temporarily alive. And then –
– you'll have proven your utility. The ministry will be keen
to make further use of you. And I know – factually – that
they need men like you. Men of your particular . . .
sensitivity.

Beat.

Darren   You don't have to do this.

Kelly   I do, or I'll be killed.
The quarantine order has already been stamped and signed.
My controller keeps it in a briefcase which never leaves his
side.

Darren   You don't want to do this.
You –

Kelly   – what?

Darren   You like them.

Kelly   I like them?

Jesus Christ.
I like them?
If that was fucking all . . .

Beat.

I would drown cities.
I would feed poison to children, then sit with them and
explain exactly how the toxin worked, even as it burned into
their organs.
I would paint your body with gentle acid that did not kill
you but let me peel your flesh away – the white, the pink,
the red – till only your bones remained.
All of this.
All of this and more.
To have one of them look at me
And not turn away
Not draw back
Not gag in disgust
For even a few seconds.

Beat.

And that is why we can't have these
Fatally radiant creatures
Walking round the place.
Reminding us how clumsy

Darren   and mean-spirited

Kelly   and graceless

Darren   and cowardly

Kelly   and shapeless

Darren   and flabby

Kelly   and foul we all are.

Beat.

Do you see?

Darren (*looks at her*)   I see.

But . . . if you met them –

Kelly *looks at him.*

Darren   – if you spoke to them –

Kelly   Don't.

Darren   – if you found out what they were like.

Kelly   We can't have them making us feel contempt for our lovers
And shame for our children
And hate for our parents and . . . hate for our selves.

Beat.

But what we could do is.

Beat.

We. You and I.
We could have them.
Before we kill them.

Beat.

Darren   He wouldn't touch you.

Kely   Not ordinarily.

But it's amazing what a man will bring himself to do if he believes his actions will preserve a woman's life.

Darren   And I don't want her. Not like that.

Kelly   You think you can't have her.
That's slightly different.
But you can.

Beat.

And you might as well, 'cause she's going to die anyway.

Beat.

Or, I have you taken in.
I do what I want to the man.

I let a squad loose on the girl.
Who do you think will be gentler with her?

Darren *doesn't answer.*

Kelly   You can have her.
You can . . . find out what she is like.

Darren *looks away.*

Kelly   Will you take me to them?

Darren *doesn't answer.*

Kelly   Darren.

Beat.

Darren *looks up at her. Nods.*

Kelly *slowly smiles.*

Darren *stares at her; then.*

I led her down towards the harbour.
I didn't know quite how to go about it.
I put my arm round her.
Round the back of her neck.
I – played with her hair.
She shivered at my touch.

Kelly   Once they're gone, and you're safe
We can –
I don't want to kill them either
But given everything
Given that they're dead anyway.
Then once they're gone
We can be together
And – we can treasure them
We can share the memory of the time we had with them

Darren   I played with her hair, and she shivered.
Not in excitement. Obviously.
She shivered and then fought it down
I watched her fight it down, and smile,

Steel herself,
And lean in towards me,
And –

Kelly   They'll live on, in a way, through us.
That'll be nice, won't it: to keep them alive a little.

Darren   It will.

Kelly   We'll never have to be alone.
I can be with you, and you can be with me,
And when we're – together – it won't matter you're thinking
about being with her
Because I'll be thinking about being with him.
You won't have to hate yourself for wanting one of them
'Cause I'll be wanting the exact same thing
But we'll never betray each other
We won't be able to
Because they'll all be dead and rotted and gone.

Darren   I watched her fight her shiver down,
Smile, and steel herself, and lean in towards me,
Her eyes closing, her lips just apart –

Kelly *cries out.*

Darren   I gripped her hair and pulled her back from me.
She started crying so I –
– I held her, by her hair, so she couldn't move or duck out
the way.
I hit her face.
She cried louder
So I kept hitting her
She quietened down and went all limp.
I let go her hair and – she just stood there,
She didn't try to run or nothing.
I didn't know what to do next.
There was this pole, like this iron pole with a hook that the
fishermen use for snagging the nets and lifting them out the
water.
She was just standing there, shivering.
I grabbed this pole and I hit her with it

I hit her in the face
And her jaw came apart
Teeth everywhere
Blood bubbling up from her mouth
She staggered back
And I hit her again
She staggered again, back towards the edge of the quay.
I kept hitting her
Knocking her back a few feet every time
Until she was right on the edge
I stuck the end of the pole in her belly
And just shoved.
She went flying off into the water.
It was like the water woke her up a bit
She started struggling and flapping around
Trying to stay afloat
Every time she went under I prayed that would be it
But she kept dragging herself back to the surface
So in the end I got the pole again and when she bobbed up the next time
I threw it at her.
And that was it.

Beat.

I stood there at the side of the quay
Watching to make sure she didn't come up again.
Gradually the water calmed itself down.
I could see my reflection.
I could see myself.
I could see: a man staring into the water, praying and praying that a girl was drowned.

Scene Seven

Tara (*beat*)   Hello.

Darren   Hi.

Tara   Are you . . . all right?

Beat.

Darren   I've just been for a walk. Down by the quay.
Cleared a few things up.

Tara   Okay.
I thought you were going to meet
the buyer.
And you were going to get us some food.

Darren (*beat*)   Yes I was.
But she didn't turn up.
She . . . I don't know.
I think the cops got her.

Tara   We're virtually out of water.

Darren   She'll be dead by now.

Tara (*looks at him*)   Her family can have my deepest
sympathies.

Darren   She's still –
I don't like it that people deal in your teeth and your hair
and –
Julian pulled it from your mouth but you've forgiven him
for that /

Tara   / He was just doing . . .

Darren   . . . what he had to do.

Beat.

How is he.

Tara   Worse.
I think he opened the wound again
When he –

Darren   – did what he had to do.

Beat.

I'll go and check on him /

Tara   / He's asleep, you should just leave him.

Darren   All right.

Beat.

Tara   I'm sorry about the girl. The buyer.

Beat.

Darren   She was fleecing me.
I'd've paid a million times what she did even to touch your hair.

Tara *stares at him.*

Darren   Oh God, I didn't mean –

Darren (*beat*)   I didn't mean I wanted to touch your hair, or anything like that.
I just meant – she wasn't paying enough.
Not that there's a price that would be enough.

Tara   Darren . . .

Darren   Because your hair should just stay on your head.

Tara   Darren: it's okay. (*She smiles.*)

Darren (*smiles back*)   You shouldn't worry about Julian.

Tara   I know, he's going to be fine.

Darren (*beat*)   Yes he is.
He's got a constitution like a . . . horse. If that's what you say.

Tara   I think you can say that.

Darren   Then that's what he's got.

Tara   He's got faith, is what he's got.

Darren   And . . . you haven't.

Tara *shrugs. Beat.*

Darren   What?

Tara   I almost missed him.

Darren *looks at her.*

Tara   I wouldn't have seen myself with a guy like Julian.
In the long term.
Not before all this.

Darren   I can't –
I'm –
I'm very surprised to hear you say that.

Tara   Before things went to hell
I was
Apt to be distracted.
By pretty faces on the street.

Beat.

I could have just . . .

Darren   . . . passed him on the street.
Never looked twice.

Tara   I'd have looked twice.
He's quite striking.
I'd've looked. And I'd've touched. And I'd've taken.
But I might've just
Discarded him.
In the ordinary run of things
And never had a clue –

Darren   – what his heart looked like.

Tara   What was inside him.

Darren   There are blessings that come heavily disguised.

Tara   Yes there are.

Beat.

Tara (*looks at* **Darren**)   What the fuck are you doing?

Darren (*looks at* **Tara**)   I was
Trying to comfort you /

Tara   / Get the fuck away from me.

Darren   I'm sorry.

Tara *looks at him.*

Darren   I thought you –
I thought you were trying to tell me something.

Beat.

Tara   I was trying to tell you
How much I love –
How lucky I am to have found him.

Beat.

Darren   Of course you were.

Tara   What did you / [think]

Darren   / I'm going to check on / Julian

(*He watches her; turns to* **Julian**)   And how is Julian doing?

Julian   I'm –
I was dreaming.

Darren   Oh yeah?

Julian *nods.*

Darren   What were you dreaming of, Ju?

Julian   I dreamed – the sand on the beaches was ground human bone.
I dreamed the mud at the bottom of the ocean was a compost of hearts and brains.
I dreamed someone tried to raise the dead and the bodies were all mixed up, the sand was suddenly alive and started to move, the mud at the bottom of the oceans suddenly itself alive and didn't know what it was but knew that it was in pain: and it lived just long enough to scream before the ocean crushed it.

Darren (*looks at him*)   And . . . what do you think that means, Julian?

Julian (*looks back at him*)   Do you think it means something?

Darren (*shrugs: then*)   I'm fine, by the way. And thanks for asking.

Julian (*looks at him*)   Did you meet the buyer? Did you get food?

Darren   She didn't turn up.
Citizens: what can you do?
You certainly can't – depend on them.
You can't trust them.

Julian   Do you . . . know anyone else we can sell to?

Darren   They're fairly replaceable. I'm sure there'll be another one along soon.

Julian   Good, that's a / relief . . .

Darren   / So this dream: it's troubling you.

Julian (*beat*)   A little.

Darren   You don't know what it means.
Its meaning hasn't been revealed to you.
You find you're lacking an answer.

Julian   I suppose it seems . . . quite –

Darren   – apocalyptic?

Julian   Yeah.

Darren   Yes that's right. I'd've said that.
Though obviously I wouldn't until you had.

Julian (*looks at him*)   Darren.
What's going on?
What's up with you?

Darren *looks at him.*

Kelly   I'm lost.
I'm lost, and it's dark.
I'm sinking. I can tell that much.
I'm sinking, and I've already gone deeper than the sunlight ever does.

There are monsters all around.
Some grey, and sleek, and full of teeth.
Some with tentacles and poison.
They're fighting.
They're fighting over me.
While the monsters fight there are smaller nightmares
Quivering jelly things attach themselves
To my face, my arms,
Semi-digesting me before they suck me in.

Beat.

Darren (*beat*)   It's nothing.
I'm fine. I'm sorry.

Julian *looks at him.*

Kelly   I've lost an arm. A grey thing swooped down and
tore it off.
The jelly creatures push their stomachs into the wound
Turning dark brown as my blood drains into them.

Darren   It's not nothing.
There's a problem.
Because the buyer didn't come, because she let me down.
I've got no money.
I couldn't buy anything.
We're out of clean water.

Julian   We've got none left?

Darren   We're almost out.
We've just got my ration.
I was wondering – should I give it to you, or should I . . .

Julian   You give it to Tara.

Darren   You're sure.

Julian   Of course.

Darren   I thought you would be.
I'll give my ration to Tara.
We'll drink the stuff from the taps

The stuff that rots your brain and eats your belly.

Julian   You don't mind, do you?
Giving up your ration for Tara.

Darren   Me?
Of course not.
Of course I should give up my ration for Tara.
I'd give up anything for –
that's only fitting.
That's only right.

Scene Eight

Tara   He's getting worse.

Darren *doesn't answer.*

Tara   I think he's got a fever.

Darren *doesn't answer.*

Tara   He needs food. Medicine. Clean water, at least.

Darren   There's none here.

Tara   No.

Which is why you have to go and get some /

Darren   / I can't go out.

Tara   What?

Darren   I went out.
The last time I went out.
I couldn't bear it.

Tara   He's going to die.

Darren   Oh, yes.

Tara   He's going to die unless you do something.

Darren   You go, then.
You go, get medicine, get water.

Beat.

Tara   Obviously I can't.

Darren   If you can't, how can I.
We're the same.
I took you in, I sheltered you, and now we're the same.

Tara *looks at him.*

Darren   Or is that wrong?

Beat.

Tara   No, it's right.
We're the same.

Beat.

And I'd go if I could.
But I can't.
So you have to.

Darren (*looks at her*)   The last time I went out.
I ended up down by the quay.
I saw my reflection.
I saw what I looked like.

Kelly   I'd have killed you in a second.
I'd've done exactly the same thing.
If it meant I could really have one of them.
That would be only . . . fitting.
That would be a right thing to do.
So'll all forgive you.
As long as it's not just –
– the same old story:
We turn on each other for want of them.
We chew each other up, for want of them.
And yet to them we're just –
– by-standers, shopkeepers, office dwellers,
fetchers, carriers, runners of errands
Shoulders to cry on, sidekicks, best friends,
But never worthy of serious consideration.
Not in that way.

Beat.

I'll understand.
We all will. /

Darren   I don't think I can go out there again.

Tara   You have to.

Darren   I don't think you're taking my concerns seriously
enough.

Tara (*beat*)   I am taking you seriously.

Darren   I don't think you've given any thought to how
much I've risked.

Tara   We don't need to give any thought to how much
you've risked. We know. We live it. We never had a choice.

Darren   Not that you'd have taken it.

Tara   If we had *any* choice, we'd have taken it.

Darren   If you could have chosen to be like us.
To be so much less.
Would you?

Beat.

You see.
Even now.

Tara   It's not like there's any huge difference between us.

Darren *looks at her.* **Tara** *looks away.*

Darren   At least before you came along
I had my own kind
as clumsy
and mean-spirited

Kelly   and graceless

Darren   and cowardly

Kelly   and shapeless

Darren   and flabby

Kelly   and foul

Darren   as they were.
I had them.
They were mine.
I wasn't ashamed among them.
I am now.

Beat.

Tara   Well, that's just a lie.
That's a lie.
You told us.
You told us you'd stopped leaving the house.
You told us you couldn't bear to open the door.
You were ashamed all along.
And you fucking should have been.
Not 'cause of shapeless, or flabby, or clumsy:
But because of death squads, and quarantines, and factories
for the safe disposal of the bodies.
It was when we came, you managed to face them again.
Because you knew you weren't part of that.
So now get up.
Get out there.
Get the fucking medicine

Darren *looks at her.*

Tara   Show me you're not part of that.

Darren *looks at her. Looks to* **Kelly**.

Kelly *looks back at him.*

Darren   Death squads, and body factories – I never
wanted that.

Tara   No.

Darren   I'm not like them.

Tara   No.

Darren   I'm like you.

Tara   You, me, Julian; we're the same.

Kelly*looks to* **Darren**. *Looks away.*

Beat.

Darren   Show me.

Tara *looks at him.*

Darren   Show me I'm the same as Julian.

Beat.

Tara   What I remember is:
The precision of it.
His use of angles.
He put his arms round me,
Lifted me off my feet,
Lowered me down to the floor.
I bent at the waist.
I bent so my body was an L-shape.
The bend was at an angle of almost exactly ninety degrees.
He then pushed against my shoulder,
Till my back, my neck, my head were all on the floor.
I was flat against its surface.
He parted my legs at this point.
Still flat against the floor
But parted: the angle was I would say
Fifty degrees.
Then he crouched at one side
Slid his arm under my knees
And lifted them up
So on the horizontal plane my legs stayed parted
At around fifty degrees
But they now were also raised into the vertical plane
The angle of the bend at my knees was I would say
Around a hundred and ten degrees. Maybe a hundred and
fifteen.
After that –

(*To* **Darren**)   Do you feel . . . better about yourself now?
Do you feel . . . more able to bear things?

Julian *comes awake.*   Tara.

Tara   I'm here.

(*To* **Darren**.) There. Did that –
– do you feel better about yourself now?

Kelly   Did that –
– was she worth it?
Was she worth . . . me?

Darren *looks at them.*

Julian   Tara.

Tara   I'm here, sweetheart.

Julian   Tara, where are you?

Tara   I'm right here, sweetheart.

Julian   I woke up and you weren't with me.

Tara   That must have been a dream, sweetheart.

Julian   Are you sure?

Tara   You know that if ever you wake up and I'm not
here, then that's just a dream. I'm always here with you.

Julian   So . . . where are you now, then?

Tara (*beat*)   I'm here.

Julian   You don't . . . you look different.

Tara (*beat*)   We had to cut my hair. For food.
We had to pull my teeth. For water.

Julian (*beat*)   That'll be it, then.

Tara   Let me hold you, then you'll know it's me.
Then you'll know I'm here with you.

Julian   Yes, if you hold me then – (*he pulls up; looks at her.*)

Tara   What?

Julian   This is – a dream, isn't it.

Tara   No, sweetheart . . .

Julian   It must be.

Julian *approaches her. Reaches out to touch her. Draws back.*

What's happened to you?

Tara (*beat*)   Nothing.

Julian   What have you done?

Tara   Nothing.

Julian   Where have you gone?

Tara *looks at him. Turns away from his gaze. Beat.*

Tara   We've got no clean water.
We've got nothing left to eat.

Beat.

If you're feeling light-headed.
If things feel a little unreal.
It's because we have no food or water
And our bodies need these things to survive.
And Darren didn't feel
It was appropriate he go out and fetch them for us

Julian (*looks from* **Tara** *to* **Darren**)   Now I see then,
don't I.
Now that's all very clear.
Now I know how to fix this.

Tara   What are you doing?

Julian   I've been lying in my sick-bed far too long.
I've been letting you cope
I've been letting you get on with things,
And now you've . . . adapted to your surroundings.

Darren   He drags himself up from the bed.

Julian   If you want something done –
– that's fine.

Tara   What I need done is –
– what I need is a moment.
I need: your breath on the back of my neck.
I need the world to close in around me
And be full of love . . .

Julian *looks at her.*

Darren   I could –
I would do that for you.

Julian (*looks away*)   I'll go and fetch the food, and the water, and –
If we need saving.
If there needs to be action.
That requires a certain kind of person.
– I shouldn't have let you . . .
It's fine.

Tara   Julian.

Darren   He squeezes past her
Coming close but not close enough to touch.
He runs up the stairs.

Tara (*to* **Darren**)   Will you stop him?

Darren   But – this is what he does.
He brings you here.
He delivers you to me.
And when I fail.
When I prove myself not to be enough
He goes and sorts it all out.
Because he – will not fail.
He is proud, and heroic, and strong,
And radiant, and pure
And above all, untainted by shame.
He doesn't exist in the same world as me.
In the same world as us.

Tara *looks at him.*

Julian God, what a relief to feel the breeze again.

Darren She runs into the hall.

Julian Tara, get out here.

Darren She takes one step beyond the doorway.

Julian Sunshine. Sunshine on my skin . . .

Darren And then she pulls up hard.

Julian Get out here and feel it, just for a moment.

Darren She pulls up hard when she sees – the citizens.

Julian Tara. Come on.

Tara They –
They crowd around him.

Darren They – are afraid to touch him for a while.

Julian You see?
You see?
They won't even lay a finger on us.
It's all just stupid.
There are millions of them.
A handful of us.
We're not a threat to them.
We could be – the jewel in their crown.

Beat.

Tara.

Darren A woman reaches out, holds her hand up to his
face –

Tara – but cannot quite touch him

Darren She sees the glow of his cheeks.
She sees something in his eyes.
She leans closer.
She sees – herself, in his eyes.

She sees herself –

Kelly   She sees herself tiny and twisted.

Darren   She sees her reflection.
She sees what she looks like.

Kelly   She sees herself disappear.
Into his eyes.

Darren   And she –

Tara   – she reaches out.
She reaches out
To fetch herself.
She reaches out with her thin and bony fingers
She reaches deep into his shining eyes.

Darren   He falls.
Face down.

Tara   The circle closes around him.
They kick and stamp
They're treading him into the ground.
Someone comes with paraffin.
They pour it on.
They set it light
And as it burns, they're –

Darren   They're joking.

Joking it's their first whiff of roast meat since rationing
began.
Joking that if the flames leave anything behind, they might
well tuck in.

Julian   Tara, help me, please.

Darren *looks at* **Tara**.

Julian   Tara.

Tara *doesn't respond.*

Darren   They're watching Julian's body.
It's crackling and sizzling on the floor.

His arms fly up.
I'm praying it's just a reflex, a reflex response to the burning
of nerves, that he's not actually still alive and –
– I can see a ragged hole in the palm of his hand,
Where a stick or a heel has stamped straight through the
charred skin and bone, and come out the other side.
A little kid runs up to the circle, finds his mum amongst the
crowd, curls himself around her leg.
The kid watches for a while.

Then he darts forward, swings his foot back, gives the body
the biggest kick his muscles can manage.
His mum . . . smiles at him, and pats him on the head.

Scene Nine

Darren   What we know now is
You can bear to be touched by me.
Maybe you didn't exactly like it
But I think that was because Julian was still around.
You felt guilty.
You were bound to.
But: you were only doing what you had to do
To save his life.
Not to save it, then:
But to make his last hours here
As comfortable as possible.

Beat.

We shouldn't let the uncertainty
Of that first experience
Contaminate future experiences we might have together.

Tara   You dreamed about this. About having one of us.
You dreamed: that one of us would find you charming.
Your hooded eyes.
Your withered limbs.
Your stooped back.
Your need for constant reassurance.

Your whining.
Your inability to dress.
Your awkwardness at table.
We might well.
We might well find that charming.

Darren   I never dreamed of /

Tara   / We might well prefer that to clear eyes and ready smiles and hearts not filled with hate.

Julian   What is this place?

Kelly *shrugs.*

Julian   Who are you?

Kelly   I – (*Shrugs.*)

Julian   We're deep in a valley.
A riverbed dry before us.

Kelly   Not a riverbed –

Julian   – the sea.

Kelly   The sea after the ocean has drained away.

Julian   The mountains rise and surround us, their tips covered in dirty snow –

Kelly   – or swallowed by black and grey clouds –

Julian   – it's hard to tell, everything here is shades of black and grey, fading up towards white but never quite managing it.

Kelly   The sky flickers. Sheet lightning.

Julian   The earth is mud and ash.

Kelly   But – in the distance –

Julian   – a light.

Julian   We float up the mountain, and we reach a cave.

Kelly   We follow the cave into the mountain.

Julian   The cave narrows till it's just a crack

Kelly   Through the crack there's –

Julian   Heat and light. Flames.

Kelly   Inside the fire there are –

Julian   – figures.

Kelly   There are people in the flames.

Julian   Their eyes and skins and hearts made of fire.

Kelly   It hurts to look at them.

Julian   We back away, back to the mouth of the cave

Kelly   But when we look out into the valley

Julian   We can't see anything at all. Our eyes are used to the light. Outside the cave, there's just an endless, featureless dark.

Kelly   When we look back into the cave, there's just fire that burns our eyes.

Beat.

Darren   I never dreamed of having one of your kind.
I only dreamed of – an angel who would come to save me.
And now you're here.
Now you're here to stay.

Tara *looks at him.*

Darren   Oh . . . no.

Tara   The door swings open.
I step out: my skin seems to crackle and tighten in the sunshine.
I walk across the street.
I kneel: the pavement is stained with blood and ash.
I reach out. I stroke the ground where he fell.
I wait.
I wait for the punches and kicks.
And . . .

Nobody looks at me twice.
People are shouting.
The sea walls have cracked.
Water is rising over the city.
People are running and I – run with them.
The crowd sweeps down to the harbour.
The far-speaker is telling us to stay back.
But people want to see
They want to know how it looks, how it feels
The streets around the quay have flooded already
The crowd falls silent: the wind disappears
For a moment, the water is flat and calm
I catch sight of myself.
I see my reflection.
The ruined mouth, the haunted eyes.
There's a shout behind me.
A tone I recognise.
A cop.
I see the uniform coming for me through the crowd
I see his arm reach inside his jacket,
I hear the crack of the holster coming open
He stops. He takes aim.
I turn to face him.
He looks away: he lowers his gun.
I'm sorry, ma'am, he says.
Just, from a distance, you looked a little like –
He dries up.
I'm sorry, he says. Please, you need to get to high ground.
(*To* **Darren**.) What've you done to me?

Darren   I've saved you.
We're the same now.
I've saved you.

Kelly   I can just make out your face: an outline at first, but
recognisably a human face. I move closer and –

Julian   Your left arm is missing.
Tendons hanging loose.
Your body ends at your belly button. Tubes and organs

hang down like a skirt.
Your jaw is broken. Your mouth ruined.

Kelly   There are scars. Burns all over your face. Your eyes
are gone. Your lips are blisters. Your nose is just a bone.
Tufts of scorched hair poke up from your scalp.
And in your hand, a hole burned right through.

Beat.

Look at us.

Beat.

We could run into the flame and be gone.

Julian   We could go into the valley and be voices in the
dark.

Kelly   Or we could stay at the mouth of the cave.
With light enough to see our faces.
And shadow enough to hide our scars.

Beat.

Darren   I did what I had to do
To save you.

Tara *looks at him; looks away. Beat.*

Kelly   Time begins to pass again.
We know because: a moon appears
and circles the sky.

Julian   A child comes.
A little . . .

Kelly   . . . girl?

Julian   A little girl.

Kelly   And when the moon rises in the sky
She asks where this ball of silver came from,
And where is it going, and can she go there too.

Julian   We tell her the moon is a garden, a heaven,
A home for the world's last treasures

A garden we hid in a stone, and threw up to the sky
To keep it safe when the seas rose.
We tell her how every day the moon comes closer
And soon it will fall and crack open the ground
Water will run again across the bed of the ancient sea
Life will start again, and spread across the land.

Kelly   You stretch up your arm, you uncurl your fist,
The moon is framed by the hole in your palm.
And our little angel shouts in delight, her eyes gleam and
blaze
To see her daddy hold the moon in his hand.

Printed in the United States
92043LV00001B/17/A